The Creative DRAWING WORKBOOK

IMAGINATIVE STEP-BY-STEP PROJECTS

Barrington Barber

ARCTURUS

This edition published in 2017 by Arcturus Publishing Limited
26/27 Bickels Yard, 151–153 Bermondsey Street,
London SE1 3HA

ISBN: 978-1-78428-577-7
AD005532UK

Printed in China

CONTENTS

INTRODUCTION

This book is about developing a thoughtful, creative approach to drawing that will bring you not only pleasure but also the ability to produce distinctive artworks. There is a lot more to drawing than simply creating an accurate likeness of what is in front of you; it is also about selecting subject matter that appeals to you, familiarizing yourself with it and deciding how you can interpret it to make an attractive piece of work.

We shall look first at the building blocks of drawing, making simple marks and then developing these into shapes that appear three-dimensional on the page. You will see how even basic geometric shapes can be used to create interesting compositions with a sense of fun. In the second chapter we shall explore the natural world as a source of inspiration for creating decorative images. The forms and patterns to be found in nature are astounding in their variety, and you don't need to venture far to find them – often no further than your back garden. Drawing plants, stones or shells is a great way to build up your skills until you feel sufficiently confident to tackle larger subjects.

In the final chapter, I've chosen various subjects that appealed to me, either for their meaning or for their visual qualities, and shown how you can develop these from a sketch to a finished drawing and then distil the forms into a more decorative and stylized piece.

Throughout the book, I have tried to emphasize the process of drawing itself rather than fixating on results, as this will help you to focus and relax. You may be tempted to stick with the first rendition you make, but I encourage you to redraw and reinterpret subjects to see if you can take them a step further. This is never a futile exercise as you will learn something new every time you put pencil to paper.

I hope that you will find some new experiences in the drawing process with this way of approaching the craft of image-making. Good luck, and have fun!

Barrington Barber

Materials and equipment

You don't need much by way of materials and equipment to get started with drawing and in this book I've deliberately kept things simple, so as to concentrate on the process of drawing itself.

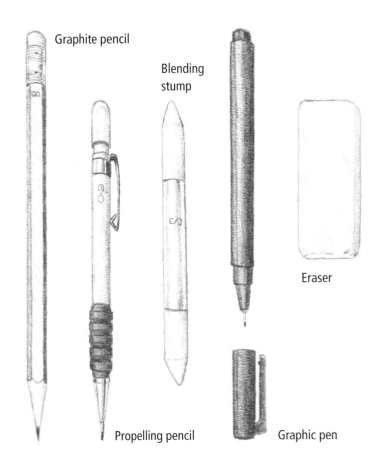

Graphite pencil

Blending stump

Eraser

Propelling pencil

Graphic pen

Graphite pencils

The most basic tool is an ordinary pencil. They are available in different grades, those marked 'H' being in the harder, paler range, not suited to our purposes here. HB is the middle of the scale then the grades run through B, 2B, 4B, 6B, 7B, 8B, each one darker and softer than the lower grade. If you want to buy just one, a B will do very well, but you may want to explore the B range further.

Propelling pencil

You will find a propelling pencil with a choice of leads very useful. The advantage of this type of pencil is that the leads are thin and produce a consistently fine line.

Blending stump

A paper stump is an artist's tool for smudging pencil marks in order to achieve a smoothly blended tone.

Eraser

Of course you will need an eraser for removing guidelines and picking out highlights. Many artists favour what is known as a putty rubber, a very soft type of eraser which absorbs the graphite and doesn't leave any debris on the paper. You can mould it into a point for tackling small areas. A hard plastic eraser is more efficient for completely removing an area of graphite but should be used with care to avoid damaging the paper. For a large area, using the putty rubber first to remove most of the graphite and then finishing with a plastic eraser takes advantage of what each has to offer.

Sharpener

You will need a good sharpener to hand, especially if, like me, you prefer drawing with softer graphite pencils in the B range; these wear down very quickly.

Graphic pen

Many of the final compositions in this book are done in graphic pen, which I find very useful in achieving a clear, formal result. Graphic pens are graded in thickness from 0.05mm to 0.8mm. I find the most useful size is 0.1mm because it gives a strong, thin line.

Paper

For your surface, you will need medium-weight cartridge paper (about 150gsm/70lb), which you can buy in sheets or in a sketchbook. A hard-backed sketchbook is most versatile as you can take it outside to draw, though bear in mind that anything larger than A3 size will be unwieldy. The drawings in this book were all done on A4 or A3 paper.

Drawing board

If you prefer a drawing board to a hard-backed sketchbook, you can buy one from an art supplies shop or, for a cheaper option, use a piece of MDF or thick plywood – a local DIY store or timber yard will probably cut one to the size you want. The best size for a board is A3 or A2, depending how large you want to draw. I usually attach the paper to the board with masking tape, but you could also use clips.

Drawing posture

Your drawing will be much more effective if you can keep your posture relaxed and free. Rather than leaning over your table, prop your sketchbook or drawing board at an angle that allows you to be more upright and balanced, which gives greater freedom to the movement through your body as you draw.

CHAPTER 1

BUILDING BLOCKS

The exercises at the beginning of this chapter are those practised by almost every artist at some time in their development, because they are the basic ways of learning how to handle and control mark-making. Next, you will build on these first principles to create abstract geometric compositions with a sense of depth. Finally, we shall look at the possibilities of pattern; what makes a pattern, how to construct a circular mandala pattern, and how you might develop creative patterns yourself.

When you start to draw, make sure that you are comfortably positioned and that you don't hold the pencil too tightly. The whole emphasis of drawing is to give all your attention to the way the pencil makes its marks on the paper, which will reward you with a sense of calm and focus.

All these exercises will help you to see how your hand movements and your eye contact with them improves the quality of the marks that you produce. It is the elegance and beauty of the marks that can make a drawing attract people's attention. By keeping to simple marks, geometric objects and patterns rather than by looking at objects in the real world, you can focus all the more on developing your technique.

Focus your attention

Your drawing will be all the more successful if you can give it your whole attention. The idea is to keep your focus on the point of your drawing tool, bringing it back every time it wanders elsewhere – which it will, frequently. However, with practice, your consciousness of your own attention span will be more alert and you will be quicker to return to your chosen point. Drawing is a good method for improving your attention span in general, as there is an obvious object – the point of the pencil where it meets the surface – and a clear indication of inaccuracies whenever your attention falters. To see the truth of this, try the following exercise.

Straight lines

Draw a line as straight as possible, giving your attention to the mark as it comes off the point of the pencil on to the paper. Any moment when your attention is not exactly on the line will show as a wobble, a stop mark or a wavering of the whole line. This way you have a record of exactly how many times your attention wavered, which will help you to keep bringing your attention back to the point of the pencil on your next attempt.

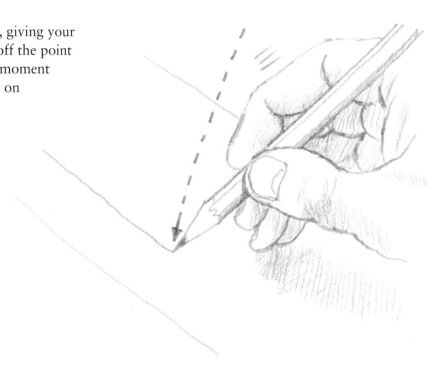

Draw vertical lines across the whole width of the page, attempting to make them perfectly straight, the same length and the same distance apart. Don't be downhearted if the lines wobble a lot, since they will show you clearly where your attention is wandering. This can only be a good thing, because until you know how to keep your attention constant you have no chance of decreasing the amount of shake in your marks.

When you have completed this first exercise to your satisfaction, try drawing another set of straight lines across the page, this time horizontally. Once again try to make the lines as straight as possible, all the same length and the same distance apart. As you will discover, this is slightly harder than drawing relatively short lines, and horizontals always seem to be a bit more tricky than vertical lines.

Circles

The next exercise is to draw a set of circles, one within the other.

Start by drawing the outermost circle as big as you need to, and as carefully as possible. It should be as close to a perfect circle as you are capable of achieving at this stage. You might need several goes before you get the sort of circle that you can work with.

Then carefully draw another circle immediately inside that one, just a little smaller. Can you keep the effect of a really good circle, as good as your first one? Then continue to draw circles within those, trying to get them right, with the same distance between them, until you reach the smallest possible.

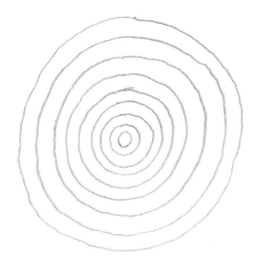

Next, draw the smallest circle first and then try to draw accurate circles outside that until you have an outer circle as large as your previous one, again keeping the same space between them. In this exercise your main guide is the central small circle, so if you can make this accurate then you may find this exercise a little easier than the one above.

While you are drawing all these marks, make sure you are not gripping the pencil too tightly. If you find your arm getting tense, consciously relax it each time. If your shoulders are hunched over, push them back and relax your posture too.

Infinity shape

Now for a slightly more complex shape; draw an infinity sign, a sort of eight shape on its side, as shown. It is called an infinity sign because it forms an endless loop, with no beginning and no end.

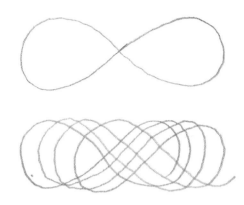

Draw it again, but this time don't quite join the lines at the end of the figure so that you can repeat the shape over and over again to produce a pattern as shown. The main thing here is to slowly build a rhythm that allows you to follow the shape smoothly across the paper. Some practice may be necessary before you can get a decent version.

Now really get going and repeat the effect over and over until you have covered the page all the way across, as in my third diagram. Don't worry if you sometimes lose your way in the line – it takes some time to become expert at this. Once again, the point of the exercise is to keep your attention on the point of the pencil as it transcribes the marks.

Zig-zag

The next exercise is to draw a zig-zag shape from left to right across the page, aiming to make each V of the zig-zag about the same width and the same length. When you have taken this across the page, draw another set over it that crosses the centre of the previous strokes, keeping everything as evenly delineated as possible. You could then try a third set and even a fourth.

Speed up

Now draw some horizontal lines across the page as before, but this time start as fast as you can and gradually slow down as you work down the page. You may have to try this several times to get the feel of it. The result of the slower lines after the faster ones is that you can really bring your attention to bear more precisely on the quality of the line. See how you get on – it should be fun.

Exercises in tone and texture

Now for some exercises on tone (light and shade) and texture. When working on these, try to keep your attention expanded to take in the whole area of the square that you are drawing over, rather than just focusing on the point of the pencil.

The first is to practise filling a square shape with tone produced by gentle movement of the pencil, back and forth in one direction. As you can see, mine is a diagonal movement made as evenly as possible. Continue until you have covered the whole area of the square.

The next, more difficult step is to vary the depth of tone in a set of squares, so that you go from the lightest tone that you can make to the very darkest, using the same method. This could take some time, as you may find that at first you cannot get a sufficiently gradual variation. As you can see, I arrived at five variations from light to dark. You may find you can stretch it out to more squares, and if so well done! The varying tone is just caused by the pressure of the hand on the pencil, but if you want more variation you could also use different degrees of pencil softness. You would then get even more variety and could increase the number of squares in your range.

Having done that you can now take the next step by starting with a very dark, almost black tone, and gradually allow it to become less and less dark until it fades out into totally white paper. Again this may take one or two tries before you can achieve it to your own satisfaction.

Now try something similar, but this time start with a dark mark and gradually fade out around the circumference to produce a sort of misty blot on the page. See how smoothly you can fade out the tone.

Circle in negative

Now we return to a circle shape, but this time you can work over it with an eraser and pencil until you feel you have produced a really good example of a circle. It is easy enough to envisage a perfect circle in your mind, but drawing one takes a bit more effort.

Once you have made a circle you are satisfied with, start to draw a dark texture around it, as shown, and continue until you have produced a dark square in which your empty circle sits. You can make this square as dark as you like, so that it really shows up the shape of the circle. You may need to try this exercise several times to get a result you are pleased with.

Creating texture

In this exercise you will be producing tonal-type images, but this time with texture instead of a solid mark. They don't have to be in a square, but I found that the most obvious and easiest shape to use.

The first one is in short scrappy marks, made by flicking the pencil lightly as I made the mark.

The second is just dots.

The third has stronger short lines crossing over each other a bit.

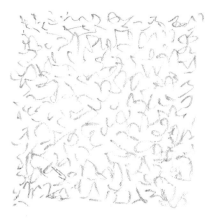

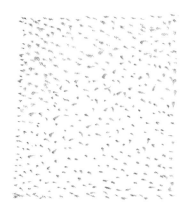

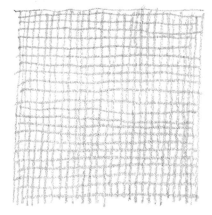

The fourth is carefully drawn verticals and horizontals with a small space between each line. As you can see, the result is like a fine network. This one needs quite a bit of concentrated attention.

Finally, a square of scribble that is done slowly and carefully, aiming to spread the final texture of crossed-over scribbles as evenly as possible over the area of the square.

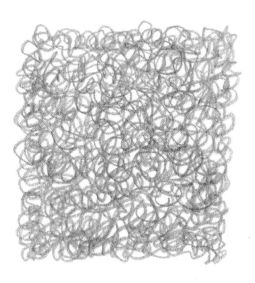

Building form

Over the next few pages we shall look at how to produce the impression of three-dimensional form. This is one of the most absorbing aspects of drawing, as you will be creating seemingly real objects on a flat piece of paper by using tone and shading to suggest roundness and solidity. First we shall look at a simple cube shape, drawn to give the impression of three dimensions.

Begin by drawing the basic cube shape.

Next, cover the two lower sides of the cube with a light tone and indicate a cast shadow that gives the impression that the light is coming from the left of the cube and is blocked from reaching the surface immediately to the right of it.

Darken the right-hand side and the cast shadow area to give a better impression of a three-dimensional object. Make the lower edges of the cube shape darker still to suggest that it is standing on a surface.

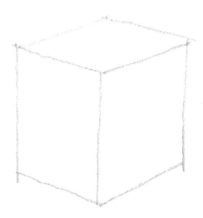 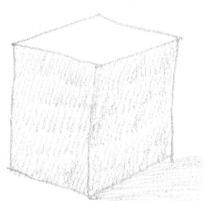 

Using tone to make an apparent sphere follows the same process of indicating light and shade.

First draw a circle, the more perfect the better.

Now make a gentle tone over about three-quarters of the area with an area of complete white in the upper left-hand quarter. Also mark in lightly a small cast shadow at the bottom to suggest the surface that sphere is resting on.

Start to darken the area which is like a crescent round the right and lower side, to emphasize the roundness of the spherical shape.

Lastly, add darker tone to the crescent area but do not darken the edges. To make it look like a sphere you need to allow for the reflective light that you always find on the outer edge of a sphere, even on the darkest side.

Darken the cast shadow where the sphere appears to touch the ground.

A more complex geometric shape

This large polyhedron shape is quite difficult to draw accurately, so you might have to try it several times. There are eight flat sides around the middle section and a flat top and bottom, with narrowing flat areas joining the two.

STEP 1
First draw the shape as well as possible. Start with a flattened circle shape at the top, then draw four lines radiating out from the bottom half of this circle. The centre line should run right down to the bottom of the shape and you can use this as a guide to construct the flat surfaces of the polyhedron.

STEP 2
Then proceed to shade in areas that would be away from the light if it were coming from the top left. As you can see, I have done seven sides in shade with a cast shadow on the right-hand side.

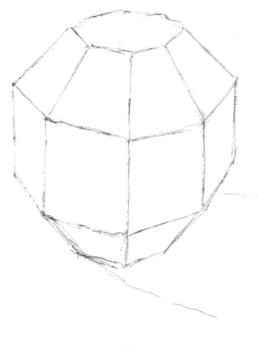

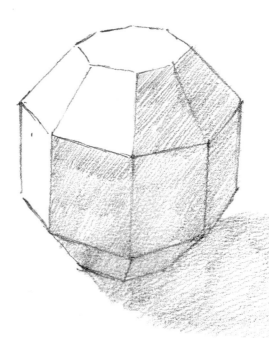

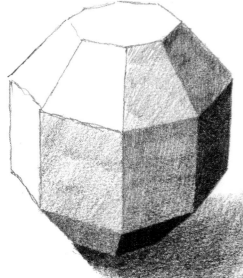

STEP 3
Then darken the right-hand top surface, the two right-hand middle surfaces and both of the lower ones. You can make the most extreme right one in the middle and the lowest one on the right almost black. Also darken the cast shadow nearest to the object.

A large tonal drawing

The aim of this exercise is to combine a set of geometric objects into a composition that appears to be three-dimensional in space. Again, the light comes from the upper left-hand side of the picture. As the composition largely consists of straight lines, using a ruler might seem a good idea but it would give a certain mechanical quality which would detract from the feel of the whole picture. Drawing it freehand is very good for practising your drawing skills, too.

STEP 1

This drawing will take a while to complete, so make sure you have a good window of time to concentrate on it fully. I have drawn two columns, one octagonal and one circular, in front of which are two cube shapes, the smaller one on top of the other. On top of the small cube is a cone and a pyramid stands on the surface next to the large cube.

STEP 2

Shading in the tone on these objects to make them appear three-dimensional and solid is quite a big task. Note the shadow cast by the small cube on top of the larger one, while the shadow from the latter covers part of the pyramid's shape.

STEP 3
Each surface needs to be a different tone to give the idea of light falling across the objects, so you will have to decide where the darker and lighter tones are. I have kept it fairly simple and have put a tone across the background space against which the objects stand out. It will take a long time to get this drawing right, so don't rush – just enjoy the building of tone.

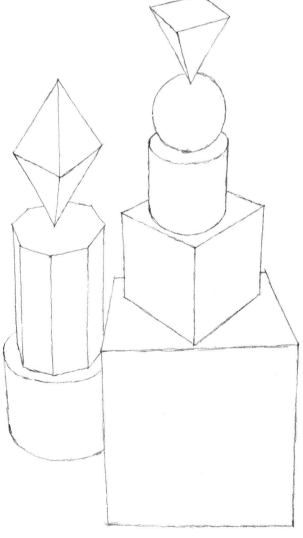

Develop your theme
This drawing is of a similar set of abstract shapes but here they look precariously balanced, giving a rather different effect to the previous one. You can start to get a feel for how to give your drawing some character, even if you are working with only abstract shapes.

STEP 1
First draw the outline with the pyramidal shapes balancing on the top of the others. Again draw them without using a ruler, because all this practice of drawing straight lines freehand is very good for your eventual technical ability.

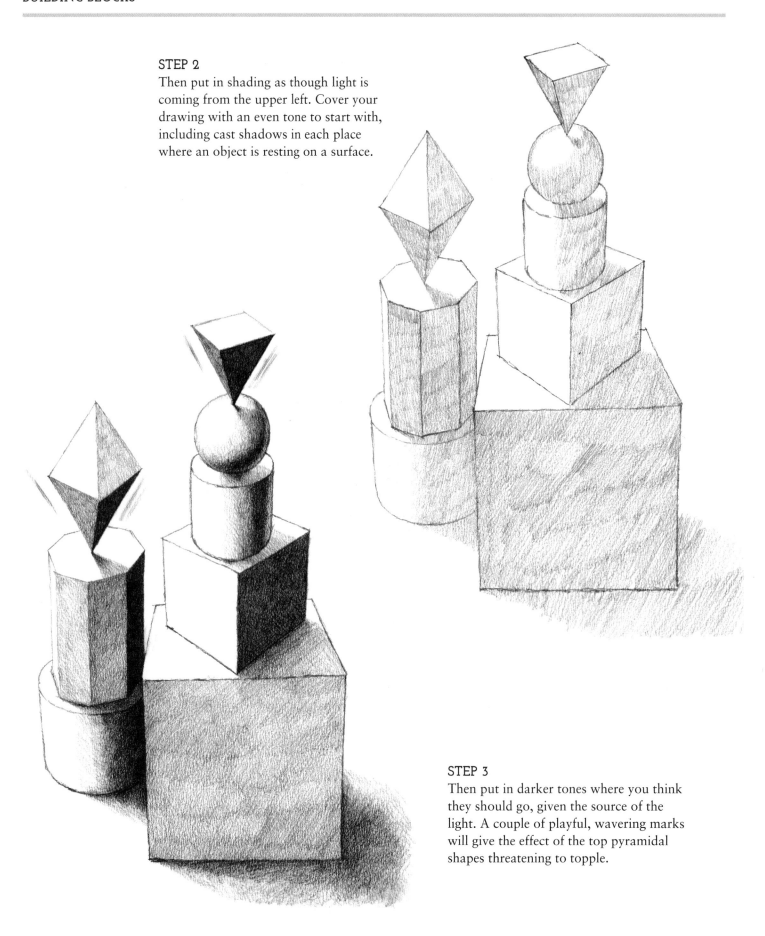

STEP 2
Then put in shading as though light is coming from the upper left. Cover your drawing with an even tone to start with, including cast shadows in each place where an object is resting on a surface.

STEP 3
Then put in darker tones where you think they should go, given the source of the light. A couple of playful, wavering marks will give the effect of the top pyramidal shapes threatening to topple.

Patterns

Throughout history, people have created patterns to decorate everything from basic household objects to monumental buildings. Whether they are very simple or highly elaborate, patterns are always based on the repetition of motifs. Drawing them can be a very therapeutic process, allowing you to build up a rhythm in your work.

To start our exploration of pattern, draw a set of five squares, all the same size. Inside these squares, draw a series of quite formal textures.

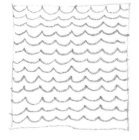   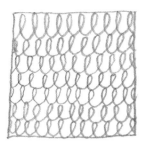 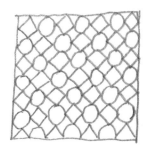

First a set of parallel wave shapes rising to small points.

Then a series of zig-zags which do not cross each other.

Next a pattern of U-shapes that give the appearance of reptilian scales.

The next pattern is formed of similar U-shapes but this time they loop along in a line.

And finally, draw a series of small circles in rows quite close together, then small diamond shapes that link the circles and join to the edges of the square.

The following simple patterns are more obviously inspired by elements of the natural world. This time draw three larger squares.

In the first, draw a watery set of lines across from edge to edge.

In the next, make some flame-like shapes, again going across from edge to edge.

Then draw some small cloud shapes across the space. If you keep all these similar in size you will see an interesting set of patterns emerging.

Now try a similar exercise but this time without the outline of the square.

First make grass-like shapes in simple tufts. You can vary the clumps of grass a little, which will add interest and allow you to fill the gaps in your pattern.

Next draw some five-pointed flower shapes. Again, varying the sizes of the flowers slightly and keeping them quite close together will give a decorative result.

Then some star shapes – don't worry if some of your stars are not geometrically accurate as this will give an attractive hand-drawn effect to your pattern.

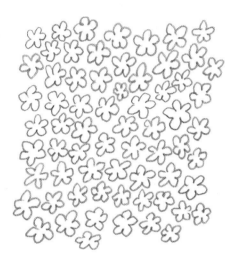

Lastly here are two examples of a formalized plant design, taking up a square space but keeping the idea of natural growth and repeating forms.

The first is just a set of curling shapes that seem to be growing out of a plant base.

The second is a more leaf-like set of marks that seem to be growing from a bush or tree. The idea is to make the small shapes interact to form a pattern.

Grid patterns

Once you have a feeling for drawing simple patterns, you can create a larger, more formal pattern based on a grid.

STEP 1
Here is a simple squared-up grid with diagonals marked in so that making a decorative pattern is quite easy. To create the grid, draw a rectangle composed of four squares across and six down then draw diagonal lines right across the grid, cutting through the centre of each square. Finally, add four vertical lines through the middle of each square.

STEP 2
In the next stage, put circles in alternate squares and arrow-shaped patterns in the other squares.

STEP 3

Draw them up in ink and erase
the construction lines to give a
simpler pattern.

STEP 4

The two larger versions of each of the
squares show how you could develop
your pattern to add more detail.

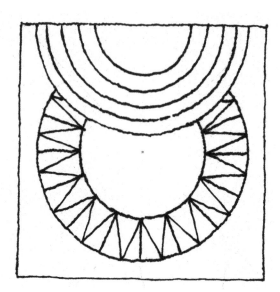

Random geometrics

Here I have put together a random pattern of geometric shapes which can become a decorative theme for colouring. When you are creating overall patterns such as this on a larger scale it is better to impart a more geometric feel to the whole by constructing them with ruler and compass. Once you have got the pattern, draw over it freehand to practise working up geometric shapes. This type of exercise can be great fun as you can develop it in myriad different ways, according to how the mood takes you. There is no need for symmetry, nor for the shapes to look like anything in particular. Try making your own pattern and see what you come up with.

Constructing a mandala pattern

The next example is a mandala pattern, which is a circular design traditionally used as a representation of the cosmos. Once you know how to construct the structure, there is great scope for experimenting with these designs. As you can see, there are several circles within each other, then the whole is divided with the radial distance, creating a system of star-like ellipses and diameters crossing the centre.

STEP 1

With a compass, first draw the outermost circle and then shorten the radius several times to produce several circles within the first one. They don't all have to be the same distance apart. Then, taking your original radius and putting the point of the needle on the circumference of the larger circle, draw across the whole shape, cutting the circle at two places. Placing the point on these two marks, draw more arcs across the whole shape then, on the last marks, draw two more arcs cutting across again. Now you will have a set of marks from which to construct straight lines dissecting the circle into even sections, all based on the centre.

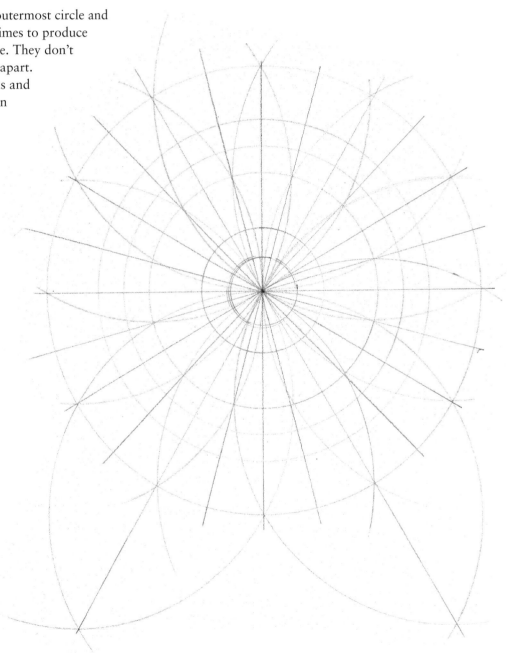

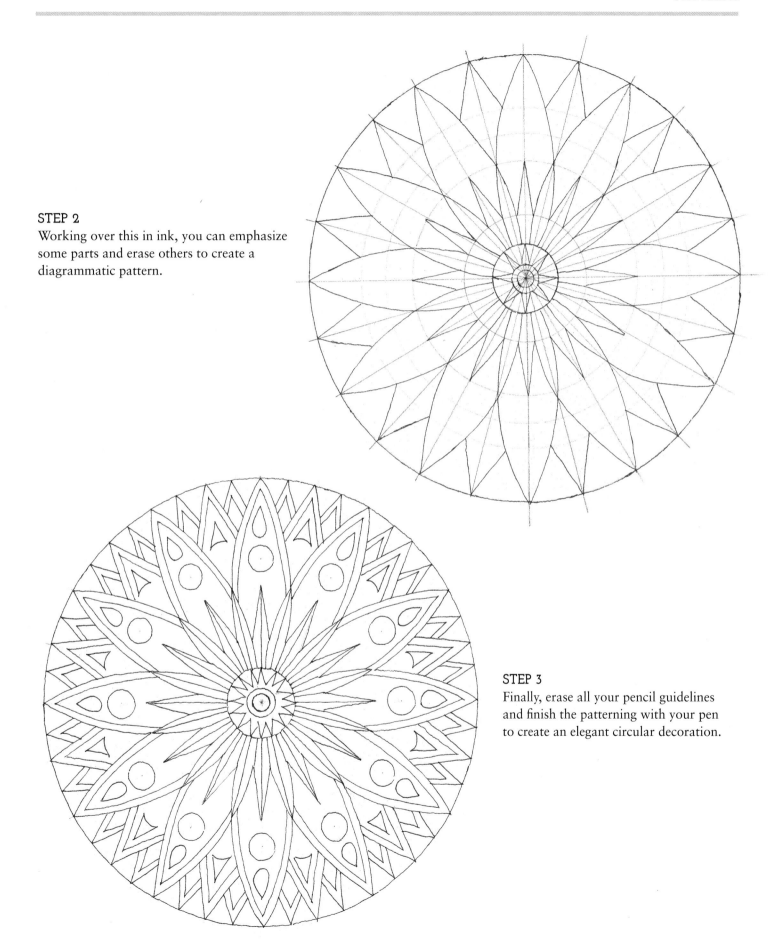

STEP 2
Working over this in ink, you can emphasize some parts and erase others to create a diagrammatic pattern.

STEP 3
Finally, erase all your pencil guidelines and finish the patterning with your pen to create an elegant circular decoration.

Spiral pattern

To finish this section, we shall look at a couple of more complex examples of how you might develop your creative pattern-making, starting with a design based on a spiral shape.

STEP 1

First, draw a spiral. This is not so easy as it sounds; you may want to use a compass to draw a series of circles with about the same distance between them. Then carefully draw your spiral by moving inwards from circle to circle, trying to make a smooth curve from one circle to the next.

STEP 2

Now all you need to do is to draw repetitive patterns and shapes at regular intervals on the spiral until you reach the centre. I used curving lines around my spiral to give it a sense of three dimensions, almost as if it were a tube.

Textured pattern

This next image is a pattern of my own invention that is neither symmetrical nor based on a single geometric shape. My intention was to produce a design with attractive decorative qualities and a more textural finished quality.

STEP 1

First of all draw the main shapes of the design, with simple flowing lines. If you are drawing your own design, be spontaneous and let your imagination guide you. Try to keep a balance of forms across the design, without making it symmetrical.

STEP 2

Now, in each part of the design, draw in very detailed and textural patterns to create something that is attractive to you and has some balance in the textured areas; for example, balance a black area on one side with a different tone on the other. Gradually build up the design until you feel that you have done as much as possible without it becoming overloaded. You don't have to finish your design in one go – sometimes it is better to take a break and come back after a while to consider your next addition to the drawing. Just go by what you feel like drawing at that moment rather than adhering to a particular plan as this allows a certain freedom of expression to come into the design.

CHAPTER 2

THE LIVING WORLD

This section of the book is about using the natural world as a source of inspiration for your drawing practice. Just the experience of communing with nature can be very uplifting; it helps us to open our minds beyond our everyday concerns, connecting us to the wider world, and so can have a calming and inspirational effect that encourages our creativity.

We shall look here at various designs taken from plants, flowers, butterflies and the elements of water and rock. If you live in a town you should be able to find all of these in your garden or local park; there is no need to be in the countryside to engage with nature. Starting from fairly realistic drawings, I shall show how they can be explored in a more formal and decorative way to create distinctive designs.

Plants have many beautiful forms that can easily be used in part or in their totality, and it is not difficult to see how these forms can be the basis of attractive drawings. Butterflies have a natural exquisiteness in their multi-coloured wings which means they hardly need to be embellished at all to produce decorative images. Looked at carefully, water offers flowing patterns created by the light and shade glittering on the surface, and rocks of many kinds can show beautiful abstract patterns. The shape of any tree seen in full bloom in summer or without its leaves in winter can give us endless sinuous shapes to use as well. The variety and complexity of natural forms make them an endlessly fascinating subject for the artist, and a constant source of inspiration.

A floral mandala

To start our investigation of natural forms we shall create a mandala as on pp.26–7, but this time integrating the shapes of real flowers into the pattern. This should give you some idea of how you can adapt the mandala template to different themes that interest you.

STEP 1

First draw some small flowers. I found mine in my local park, all of them wild flowers. I took careful close-up photographs of them to use as my basic form. Keep the drawing as clear and as simple as possible.

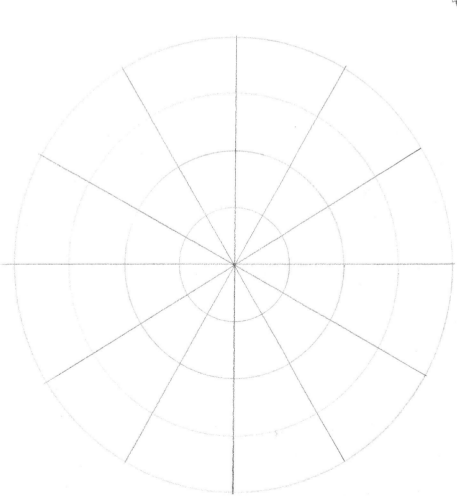

STEP 2

Next construct, as shown, a circular shape divided into four rings and twelve segments. This form is constructed in a similar way to the mandala shown on page 26, but here the distance between each circle is exactly the same and there are fewer segments.

STEP 3
Now place your flower shapes into the grid, with one flower in the middle and various versions at each layer of the circle. Note that in the inner circles I have repeated each flower motif six times, alternating them with leaves. In the outer ring where there is more space I placed a flower in the centre of each of the twelve segments of the circle, and alternated these with more flower and leaf shapes.

STEP 4
To finish, draw up the whole design in ink. Once you are happy with your design and the ink is dry, you can rub out your pencil guidelines. Finally, add in any additional details that you think fit, such as the leaf flourishes and the centres of the flowers.

Garden plants

For this exercise I took another realistic subject as the starting point: some leafy plants in my garden. The intention here is to make them into a formal, stylized drawing that still relates to their original shapes.

STEP 1
First draw the plants and surrounding leaves quite carefully, in outline, as accurately as you can.

STEP 2

The next step is to draw up the forms formally, so that they fill up the space more evenly. Using your first drawing as reference, redraw them from scratch, removing some of the very small leaves and repeating some of the more obvious shapes. I added another plant on the right to create an almost symmetrical composition.

STEP 3

Next, formalize the leaf shapes even more to create a decorative version of the original plants. At this stage I traced off the pencil drawing in pen to give it more clarity.

STEP 4

In this final drawing, the elements of the previous stage are rearranged to give a tighter format. It can be tempting to stick with your first composition if things seem to be going well, but you can often achieve a more successful drawing if you play with the elements and move away from a straightforward representation of the forms in front of you. For me, this tighter composition is an improvement. But whatever the result, redrawing a composition is never time lost, because you will gain in understanding and fluency with your pen or pencil.

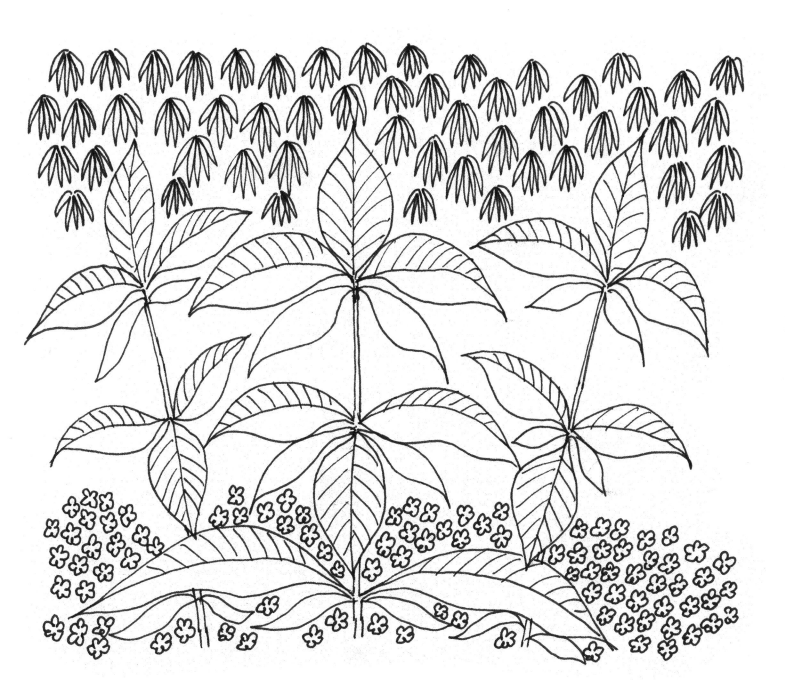

A grassy plant

I discovered this rather beautiful growth of leaves in a horticultural garden not far from where I live and thought its flourishing foliage made it a good subject for a drawing.

STEP 1
Start by drawing the arrangement of leaves as clearly as you can, noting the way they all rise out of the centre.

STEP 2
Next, add a light tone across the plant, leaving the lightest areas untouched.

STEP 3

Put in the darkest tones to give your drawing a bit more depth and liveliness. You can ignore the plant's surroundings and let it appear by itself on the page. This helps to make it look more dramatic, as though it were growing out of the paper.

STEP 4

Then, tracing off the drawing in ink, add the tones in textural forms to produce an even more powerful image on the empty page. It is necessary to take your time with this and concentrate on the mark you are making at each second. The decorative image is a potent description of growth and life.

Leaf patterns

The variety of leaves to be found in any area with a good covering of vegetation and their changing appearance throughout the seasons in temperate climates makes them a wonderful subject to study. This example is from a large grassy area that had a mix of large fallen leaves and smaller ones still in growth.

STEP 1
First, I drew a patch of ground with some larger leaf forms, grass and smaller leaves. This was how they looked without any redesign. Start your own work with this realistic approach to get the feel of the leaves.

STEP 2
Redraw them slightly more formally, moving them around to fill up the available space and create distinct areas of texture.

STEP 3

Finally, draw them all up in ink, making sure that they cover all the available space. As you can see, the grass becomes a very good form of background patterning. It is really just a set of wavy lines repeated across the background area to fill up the space between the large leaves in an attractive texture, and the smaller leaf pattern in the lower left corner performs the same function. The contrast between the dense lines of the grass and small leaves and the white areas of the large leaves is what gives this composition its interest and decorative effect.

Seashells

Now we move on to another type of natural form, that of seashells that I have collected at various times on visits to the seaside. They have very mathematical forms and require some study to get all the details correct.

STEP 1
Start with the outline shapes and main forms of the shells, making each one as accurate as possible.

STEP 2
Add all the marks and patterns on the surface, shade in the darkest areas and firm up your outlines to give the shells some weight.

STEP 3

Redraw the shells in ink and simplify them slightly, using light hatching instead of graduated shading in the darker areas. To make the task easier, you can trace your original outline drawings.

STEP 4

Redraw as many shells as you like and simplify them yet further, formalizing the shapes so that they are almost like decorations. Drawings such as this can be used as motifs in a pattern, or for colouring in.

A large tree

Trees are a wonderful source of inspiration throughout the year. Their longevity and resilience give us pause for thought and their beautiful variety of branches and leaf shapes give the artist many forms to use.

This large tree stands in a park near my house. One pleasant morning I found a good position far enough away to get a good view of it in its entirety and drew it from life.

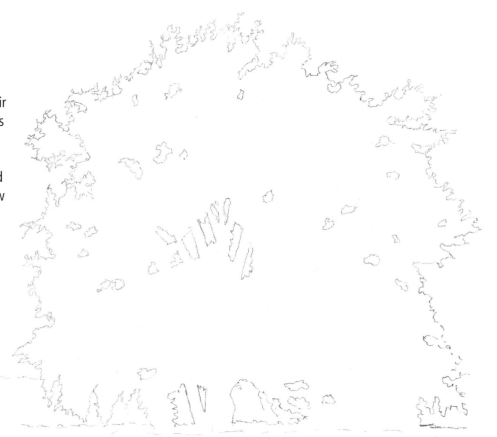

STEP 1
Start with a careful outline of the entire shape, noting the places where one can see through the leaves and branches to the sky behind.

STEP 2
Next, spend some time very carefully adding all the different textures of the leaves and branches. As you can see, I've simplified the tree greatly by drawing the foliage as blocks of tone, rather than attempting to draw each leaf separately. To help you get a sense of how the light falls on a large tree like this, try narrowing your eyes.

STEP 3

Next draw it in ink, which requires a little more simplification, showing variation in the leaf patterns. In my ink drawing I have reduced the forms of the leaves and branches to three tones or textures. For the lightest areas use just a simple line hatching, for the darker areas a more scribbly tight texture and for the very darkest areas solid black.

STEP 4

Now try an even more simplified and formalized drawing of the tree
in ink with three systems of leaf texture as before, but this time with a
slightly more decorative approach. Although this image has the graphic
appearance of a woodcut, it is in fact not so far removed from my original
drawing of the tree itself.

A tree close-up

With this interpretation of a tree I drew in ink from the start, using a much closer angle of view than in the previous exercise. This gives a real sense of the size of the tree, as well as its varying textures and forms.

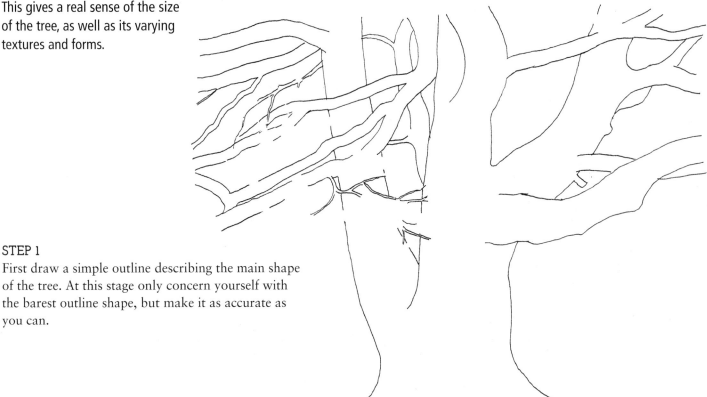

STEP 1
First draw a simple outline describing the main shape of the tree. At this stage only concern yourself with the barest outline shape, but make it as accurate as you can.

STEP 2
All that is necessary now is to fill in the various textures of the lichen-covered branches and the leaves and grass. Keep the patterns of these fairly simple, relying on the varied small shapes to produce a decorative pattern overall.

A tree trunk

This sawn-off piece of solid tree trunk had been lying in wetlands near my house for a while when I decided to draw it. It has a nicely patterned bark that shows where a bit of the outer bark has fallen off, and is surrounded by grass and leaves.

STEP 1

As the shapes created by the sawn-off branches are quite complex, first follow my outline drawing of the whole trunk. I indicated the edges of my composition with a few sketchy marks showing the grass around the log.

STEP 2

Next, begin to add tone across the drawing, including the shadow areas around the trunk. I lightly sketched the mottled-looking areas where the bark had peeled off.

STEP 3

Work up the drawing by putting in all the textures of the surfaces and the grassy surrounding ground. This will take you some time.

STEP 4

For a different approach, redraw the log with a pen and just make outlines of the areas of different textures on the bark. Formalize the patterns of the surrounding ground with little tufts of grass. Even in this simplified rendition, there is a sense of the size of the trunk and how big the tree must have been while alive.

Pebbles

Although stones might not seem an obvious subject for the artist, they lend themselves well to artistic interpretation because of the variety of their patterns. At a glance these pebbles looked grey and uniform, but on closer inspection they are covered in detail and each one is unique.

STEP 1
Here the pebbles are viewed from above so that there are no cast shadows and the distinct outline of each stone is clear. Draw them as realistically as you can.

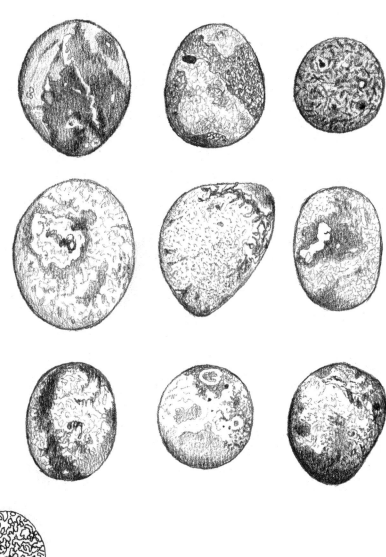

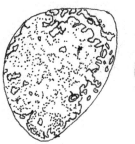

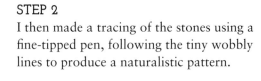

STEP 2
I then made a tracing of the stones using a fine-tipped pen, following the tiny wobbly lines to produce a naturalistic pattern.

STEP 3

Finally, you can add hatching, cross-hatching and stippling to your tracing, to bring out the patterns on the stones and give them a more ornamental look. You can reproduce drawings like these in different arrangements or integrate them into varied designs.

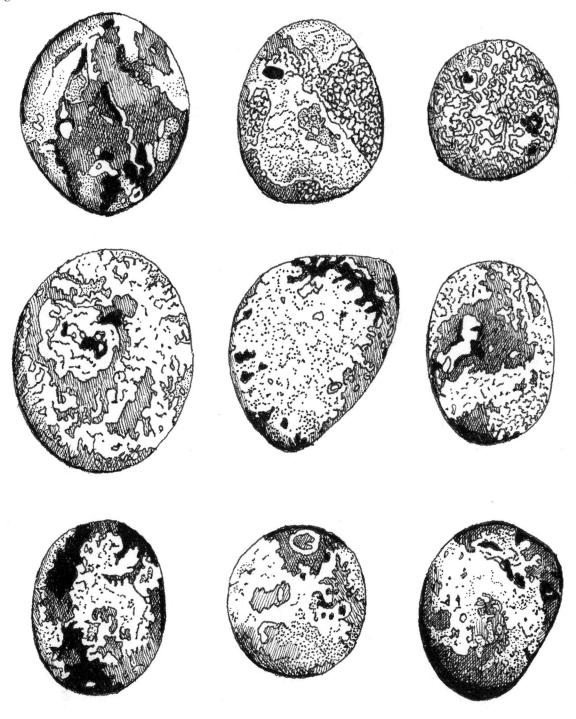

A butterfly mandala

This time we shall take butterflies as the theme for a mandala. As a subject for drawing they are very attractive with their multi-coloured wings and the shapes are so distinctive that they are instantly recognizable as a motif. It is nigh-on impossible to draw butterflies from life as they rarely settle for more than a few seconds, so I drew mine from a photograph.

STEP 1
First draw three butterflies, showing all their patterns clearly on their wings. If you are using ink as I have, use a combination of hatching, cross-hatching, dots and solid ink to show the different areas of pattern.

STEP 2

Now construct a circular grid and divide it into six equal segments, then sketch in the outline shapes of the butterflies. As you can see I have placed one in the centre, six around that and six more on the outside.

STEP 3

Next, using your initial drawings as reference, draw in all the relevant patterns of the wings in three simple textures: line hatching, dotted and solid black. This stage may take some time.

A sunset

Landscapes and seascapes are always interesting to an artist because of the immense variety of effects to be seen in the sky, sea and vegetation. A landscape can seem a daunting subject for a novice artist, but breaking it down into principal areas of tone and not attempting to draw every detail can make it much easier. I saw this view of a very attractive sunset among layers of cloud near the south coast in England.

STEP 1
First, sketch the main areas of your scene as accurately as you can. Pay particular attention to the silhouette of the greenery and the gate in the foreground.

STEP 2
Add a light tone across the drawing, leaving white areas to indicate the shafts of sunlight. You can use your eraser to define these areas.

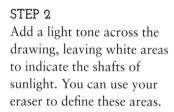

STEP 3
Now add more tone to get the best effect of the rays of the sun bursting through the cloudy sky. The key to this is using a paper stump to smudge and soften the edges of the clouds and light rays. Darken the foreground as much as possible to create a dramatic contrast between land and sky.

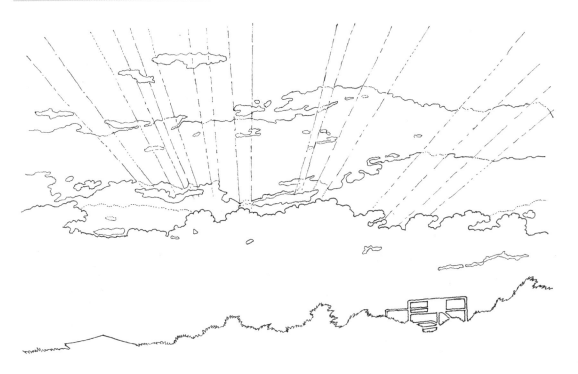

STEP 4
Then trace the main outlines of the drawing in ink to create a simplified version. Where you want a lighter line, use dotted or dashed lines with your pen.

STEP 5
Next, building on the outline drawing, add tones using repetitive patterns of hatching, cross-hatching and solid black ink. For the very palest tone of the sky, use light pencil marks smudged with a paper stump. Radiate the lines on the upper clouds to follow and emphasize the rays of the sun.

Water

It is not easy to draw water at first, but as long as you convey the feeling of liquid movement you will succeed. One of the simplest ways to do this is to take several photographs of the surface of a stream or river and then to copy the dark and light ripples as accurately as you can. What you will soon notice is that the patterns are very similar all over the surface, so the main thing is to get the feel of this repetitive swirl across the page.

STEP 1

Here I have drawn as realistically as possible some water flowing in a stream. As you can see it is broken up into waves that reflect the light and dark of the surrounding landscape and sky. You can draw them quite loosely, showing the broken texture and the patterns of the wavelets.

STEP 2

Now draw the same waves more precisely to show the different tonal patterns. This requires that you formalize each small area of tone and texture and decide how many changes of pattern that you need. I used patterns of black, dotted, and hatched pen as well as grey pencil shading.

Birds

The neat shapes of birds and their feather patterns give a very useful way to make decorative shapes. I have used good photographs of British wild birds – the fieldfare, the goldfinch, the hawfinch and the flycatcher – but wherever you live you will have plenty of avian subjects that appeal to you.

STEP 1

Start your drawing with very simple shapes to get the right proportions. Bird poses are very distinctive, with cocked heads and wide eyes, so try to capture this in your sketch.

STEP 2
The next step is to produce a more detailed drawing showing all the patterns and colours of these small creatures. Remember to leave a small area of white in the black eyes: this highlight is crucial to the birds looking alive and alert.

STEP 3
Next, make outline versions of the originals and arrange them in a neat pattern, close together.

STEP 4

Then draw them in ink, showing the divisions of colour and texture also in outline. Extend the outlines into a surrounding pattern of lines or stripes to help produce a complete design.

STEP 5

Finally, add tones and textures to your line composition. I used pen to denote areas of pattern on the birds and a uniform pencil tone in the outline pattern around the main bird shapes, but how you choose to add tone at this stage is up to your own personal preference. You can have fun varying your marks and assessing the different effects. If you want to try another approach, trace off your design and add tone again.

A heron

I came across this beautiful heron in a wetlands area near me and realized that it would make a good picture. Herons are such distinctive birds: sometimes they are poised and graceful, at other times they seem ruffled and comical. I wanted to capture the absolute stillness and alert gaze of the bird, so I took a photograph which I later used to make this drawing.

STEP 1
First draw a simple outline that gives you some idea of the overall shapes. Getting the characteristic stance of the bird is important, so don't hesitate to erase and try again if it doesn't look quite right.

STEP 2
Now work quickly over the whole picture, adding a light tone in all but the lightest areas.

STEP 3

Next, work across the whole picture, adding in darker tones and detail. The marks of the vegetation in the background can be quite sketchy as you are just trying to give an impression. Use stronger, harder marks for the cracks and striations of the log in the foreground and take your time to accurately capture this magnificent bird. As you can see, the log and the background vegetation almost camouflage it.

STEP 4

Then trace off and draw up in ink a more decorative version of the composition. Here I made a repeating pattern of scribbly lines for the background leafy area and a formal hatching of dense lines in different directions for the log. I used darker hatching around the foreground shapes of the heron and the log to make them stand out against the background.

A coastline

Here I have chosen another landscape scene, this time showing part of the southern coast of England. The contrast between the white cliffs, the vegetation on top of the cliffs, and the water lapping over the beach give plenty of scope to develop an interesting composition.

STEP 1
First make an outline sketch of the scene, showing the main shapes of the vegetation, the white cliffs, and the incoming sea.

STEP 2
Next add a light tone across the scene to identify the darker areas and give it some depth.

STEP 3

Work further on the tone in the clouds, the trees on the tops of the cliffs and the rocks and sand of the beach below, with the sea lapping gently on to it. Use formalized marks on the cliff sides and very dark areas of pencil tone for the vegetation and sea kelp; for the sea and sky, make a light tone and smudge it with a paper stump.

STEP 4

Now make another version in ink, using textures to indicate the tones of the land and sea. As before, use pencil smudged with a paper stump to make a light grey tone in parts of the sky and on the sea.

STEP 5

Take the drawing one step further, rendering the whole composition with greater formal patterning and a certain amount of simplification. As you can see, you don't have to create an exact copy of your original drawing; feel free to slightly change the shapes in order to produce an interesting composition.

CHAPTER 3

BE INSPIRED

In this section we shall look at a range of objects and scenes, both in your home and further afield, which will help you to develop your drawing style. You can find plenty of inspiration in your domestic environment if you select your subjects carefully. Choose subjects that you enjoy looking at; even if they are not obviously beautiful they will have some kind of aesthetically pleasing aspect. You can then build on the visual qualities that you find interesting to create a drawing that is not just a straightforward rendition but adds an element of your own interpretation. To break this process down, we shall look first at how to draw each subject as you see it, then how you can pare down your composition and translate it into something more imaginative.

We shall start with single objects – a candle, a bowl, a flower in a vase – and progress to more complex subjects including a formal garden and a cathedral. I hope that the range of subjects I've chosen will give you a feel for how to select themes from your own environment that accord with your interests. If there is a theme running through my selection it is one of calm, because many people find subjects such as these invite a sense of calm contemplation that is very conducive to creativity. As you progress along your path to becoming an artist, you may find your more intense moments of creativity are fired in other ways; we are all different, and the joy of being an artist is that expressing one's individuality is always encouraged.

A candle

This drawing of a lighted candle has a feeling of peaceful stillness yet the effect of the flame is to give the picture life. The flame has a connection with our ideas of light and the precariousness of life; even a simple drawing of an everyday household object can carry a message to the thoughtful viewer.

STEP 1

The first drawing needs to be a careful outline of the whole shape, as accurate as you can manage. The difficulty here will be achieving the symmetry of the object, but even if you do not get it quite right the effort of attention to the shape and form will produce an interesting result.

STEP 2

Then add a light tone across your drawing, except in those areas where there are bright highlights. Half-closing your eyes will help to identify those areas, and you can circle them lightly with your pencil before hatching in the tone. At this stage you can also sketch in an area of shade around the outside of the flame to help show its glowing properties.

STEP 3
Then you need to add the deeper tones, blending them with the mid-tones to create a smooth finish. Note how the contrast of tone on the candlestick is stronger than on the candle itself. This helps to differentiate the materiality of the metal stick with the candle's waxy finish.

Mark in some lines on the tabletop to indicate the woodgrain texture. Leave the area of the flame itself white, set against the darkest part of your background for contrast; if you smudge it, just pick out the smudge with an eraser.

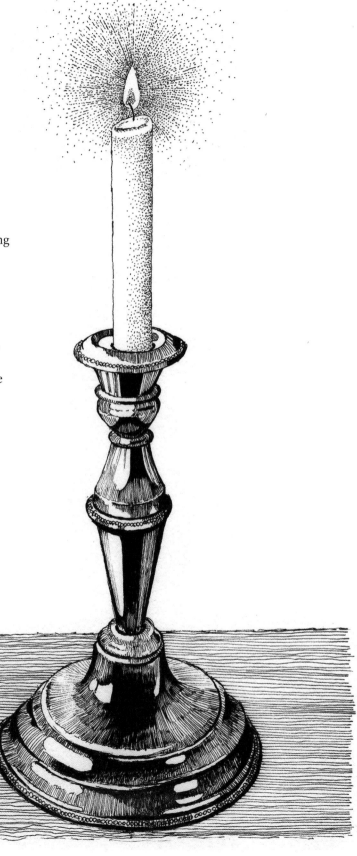

STEP 4

Finally, I traced my initial outline drawing
in ink. With a very fine-nibbed pen
(0.1mm), I built up areas of hatching,
solid black and dotted textures. The
overall effect is more decorative than
the pencil drawing, and the contrast
between bright and dark areas is greater.
This method of ink drawing requires
care and concentration. I have drawn the
line hatching on the metal candlestick
to follow the shape of each part of the
object. The stippling or dotting method
on the candle itself and to describe
the light around the flame is useful for
making less definite tone.

A Hindu statuette

This image of the god Krishna and one of his consorts seated on a peacock is a traditional ivory carving, mounted on a sandalwood base, that my father brought home from India in 1945, after the Second World War ended. Intended as an object to meditate on, it is quite small, not even as big as my hand. You can try drawing this statuette after my example, or look for an equivalent object in your own home; something familiar that speaks to you of your home and family, imbued with memories over the decades that gives it meaning for you.

STEP 1
First make a sketch of the object, taking care to get the proportions right. The plinth is the most well-defined form, so check your widths and heights in relation to that.

STEP 2
Next add tone and shading to give the effect of ivory and wood. Note how much darker the wooden base is, with the surface acting as a midtone between the two. Keeping the ivory drawn very lightly in parts helps to show the translucent quality of it. The wooden base looks much heavier, while the ivory appears to float over the top.

STEP 3

Now have a go at drawing the same image in ink, giving it a slightly more formal look. The shade on the ivory figurine is in a dotted texture to give it a more glowing effect than the wooden base. Keep all the shading very formalized to give a more ornamental effect.

A Chinese bowl

The next image is of a decorative bowl from China – a deep bowl with a lovely form. I decided that I would set it against a dark background and leave the inside white. In this way I could subtly draw attention to the real purpose of the bowl, which is to say the space inside it.

STEP 1
As before, draw the outline lightly and carefully to capture the masterful proportion and shape of the bowl. Paying attention very precisely to your efforts to get the shape right will give you some idea of the satisfaction of creating with care, as the artisan who made the bowl would have experienced.

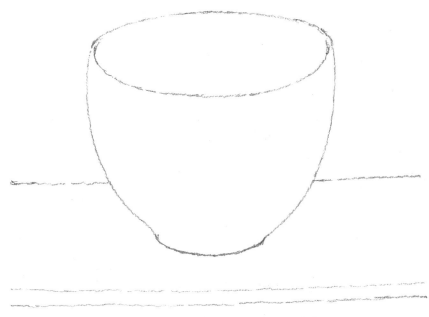

STEP 2
Then start to put in the tonal values, being careful not to make anything too dark or strong, apart from the outline of the bowl.

STEP 3
Once you have completed your pencil drawing, try to render the bowl in ink. In my version the tones are replaced by textures that are very decorative in their effect. I have used a rather strong textural device of groups of small lines to give a stronger effect to the background, which has the effect of making the more lightly textured bowl look brighter and less solid. Once again, don't let any markings on the bowl get too heavy, except for the outline.

A flower in a vase

For this drawing, I placed a single bloom of a bearded iris in a vase. I chose a simple, undecorated container as I wanted to draw attention to the complex beauty of the flower. Taking time to study a flower like this will give you the opportunity to understand and appreciate its exquisite form.

STEP 1
First draw the flower and the vase in outline, getting the distinctive shapes of the petals as accurate as possible.

STEP 2
Now add some tone, keeping it light and uniform across the whole image at this stage. The idea is to identify the main areas of light and dark and start to give body to the shapes in your drawing.

STEP 3

Now add detail and the darkest tones, which as you can see are very strong, especially on the leaf. For the undersides of the petals I chose a darker tone and on their upper parts I applied light hatching that followed their wavy forms. The darkest tones of all are on the leaf behind the stem: I applied plenty of pressure with my pencil here and worked into the tones to get them as dark as I could. Although this flower was in fact a very colourful red and yellow, working in pencil like this gives you a chance to focus on form and translate it to the best of your ability.

STEP 4
Now try an ink version which
maintains that strong dark quality
of the leaf and the dark red parts of
the petals. Keep the texture on the
vase lighter and less insistent. I used a
number 0.1 pen for the main drawing
and a number 0.8 for the very
solid blacks. On the vase a stipple
dot technique gives a lighter look,
while on the petals fine broken-line
hatching or very solid darks indicate
the variation of colour and tone.

A glass of water

A glass of water is an everyday thing that could be passed over without a thought but in fact it is an interesting subject for a drawing, suggesting calm and clarity. It shows how even the most simple objects are full of visual interest and open to interpretation with your drawing marks.

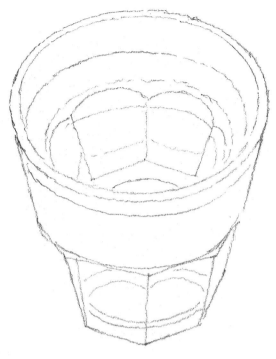

STEP 1

First draw the shape, looking down into the glass, very simply and clearly, reducing it to the fewest marks that you can make on the paper. The hardest part will be the ellipse or flattened circle of the rim of the glass – take your time to make this as accurate as you can, erasing and redrawing as necessary.

STEP 2

Now add a light tone across your drawing, including the background area. On the glass, the only areas left white are the very brightest highlights: squint your eyes to identify where these are.

STEP 3

Now work on it to add all the tones and shading
that are needed to give it a feeling of depth and
dimension, building up the tones slowly and
carefully, until the sense of its reality is observable.
My glass was placed on a metal sink which reflected
the form nicely and gave me an opportunity to
anchor it into a dark background.

STEP 4

Then draw it again, in ink this time, building
darks and midtones with careful cross-
hatching methods. The ink intensifies the
whole picture, giving great contrast between
the very darkest and the very lightest areas.
The slow build-up of texture across a dark
picture like this will require a lot of close
attention, so take your time – there is no need
to get it finished in one go.

A stained glass bouquet

With this drawing, the aim is to create a composition that looks like a stained glass window. I took various flowers and drew them in a very formalized way, simplifying their shapes. This has the effect of flattening out the images rather, which helps to make them look as though they are all on the same plane. One is like a rose, one like a lily and the third resembles a sunflower or large daisy.

STEP 1

Choose your flowers for maximum decorative contrast and arrange them in an arc shape with a border and a base shape from which they sprout. This is as much a design as a drawing of flowers, and you will need to consider how to arrange each bloom to produce an interesting combination of shapes across the whole composition. Just use your eye to produce something harmonious in a formalized shape like the one I have designed – attractive and relatively uncomplicated.

STEP 2

Draw the design in some detail, making it as decorative as you can. My initial drawing was done with a fine 0.1mm pen. Go carefully as with pen you will find it harder to correct any errors. If you make a major one you may have to start again, but for small errors a little touch of white gouache paint will do the trick.

STEP 3

Lastly, work in texture and tone to give the impression of something that might be found in a stained glass window. I used pencil for subtler shading in the leaves and stalks, as well as fine hatching and stippling in pen for variety. As you can see, all the main shapes are surrounded by a heavy ink line to represent the leading in a stained glass window.

A Bavarian woodshed

Subjects for drawing can be found anywhere, so keep your eyes peeled for sights that inspire you. This pile of logs, stacked in a shed in Bavaria, caught my imagination as the wood was so perfectly arranged it was almost like a work of art in itself. I took a photograph and used it as the basis for this drawing.

STEP 1
First make a simple but accurate outline of the various logs at different angles. The shapes might look quite odd at this stage, but take care to draw exactly what you see.

STEP 2
The next step is a more detailed drawing showing all the tones and textures in the picture. The texture of the logs can be shown with cracks and knots along their surface. Use an eraser to pick out highlights where the sun touches the log pile.

STEP 3

Now trace off your drawing and render it in ink. This produces a slightly simpler form due to the less tonal quality of the ink lines and marks; the pen line is less varied, but it has greater definition. I chose mostly vertical hatching, with some cross-hatching for the deeper shadows. Capturing the diagonal shafts of sunlight was harder in pen than in pencil, as it can only be done by leaving some areas white as highlights.

A water lily

In this image of an open water lily on a pond, I was aiming for an attractive, decorative composition rather than a representational drawing. Lilies symbolize purity, beauty and rebirth and I wanted to point to this meaning rather than focusing on realistic details. The composition is based on some photographs of water lilies that I had at home, but I made the water look darker in my drawing so that the lily was the main source of light. When you draw from photographs, always ask yourself if the image can be improved upon as far as your drawing goes.

STEP 1
First draw in the main shape as carefully as you can, keeping it only in outline. If you are adapting or simplifying an image as I did, now is the time to really think about the forms you want to show and the overall composition.

STEP 2
Next put in the tone, noting how much darker some areas of the water are than the petals of the flower. Because the water is very still, you can divide it up into areas of tone, leaving some white to show the light reflecting off the surface.

STEP 3

To take your composition one step further, trace off your first drawing and redraw it in ink, making the tones more textured and trying to keep the balance of dark and light. Here I used some line hatching for the medium tones, mainly horizontally drawn to help give an effect of the calm surface of the water. The solid black areas are around the leaf shapes to give them more definition.

A cathedral

So far in this section we have looked at relatively small subjects, but here I have chosen a building to draw – Rochester Cathedral in southern England. This might seem like a daunting task, but you don't have to draw every detail. I have shown first how you might go about making a straightforward drawing of this 11th-century place of worship and then how you can play with the various elements to make a simplified, redesigned image.

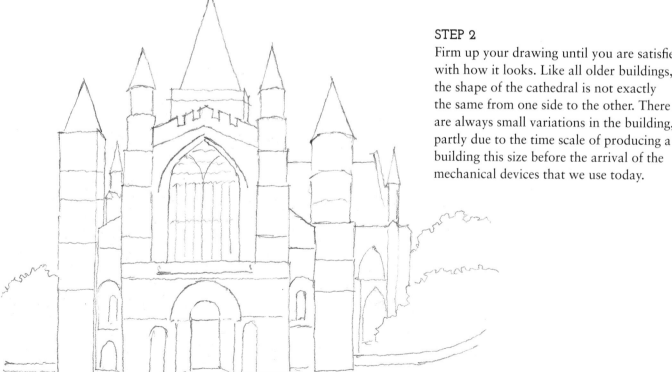

STEP 1

Draw the main shape as clearly and as accurately as you can. I stood at sufficient distance to see the main area of the cathedral and then proceeded to make it cover the whole area of the page I was drawing on.

STEP 2

Firm up your drawing until you are satisfied with how it looks. Like all older buildings, the shape of the cathedral is not exactly the same from one side to the other. There are always small variations in the building, partly due to the time scale of producing a building this size before the arrival of the mechanical devices that we use today.

STEP 3

Now draw everything in ink, putting in texture wherever it is needed. I recommend that you trace off the main shapes in the original pencil rendition to ease any drawing difficulties. Make the main lines of the structure slightly stronger than the rest. The dense texture of the vegetation on each side of the cathedral helps to bracket the shape of the building and define its depth.

STEP 4

This drawing of the cathedral rather redesigns the whole building. I simplified the shapes and moved them closer together, as well as adding the detail of the brickwork to give a more decorative effect. While it is still recognizable as Rochester cathedral, it is my interpretation of that building.

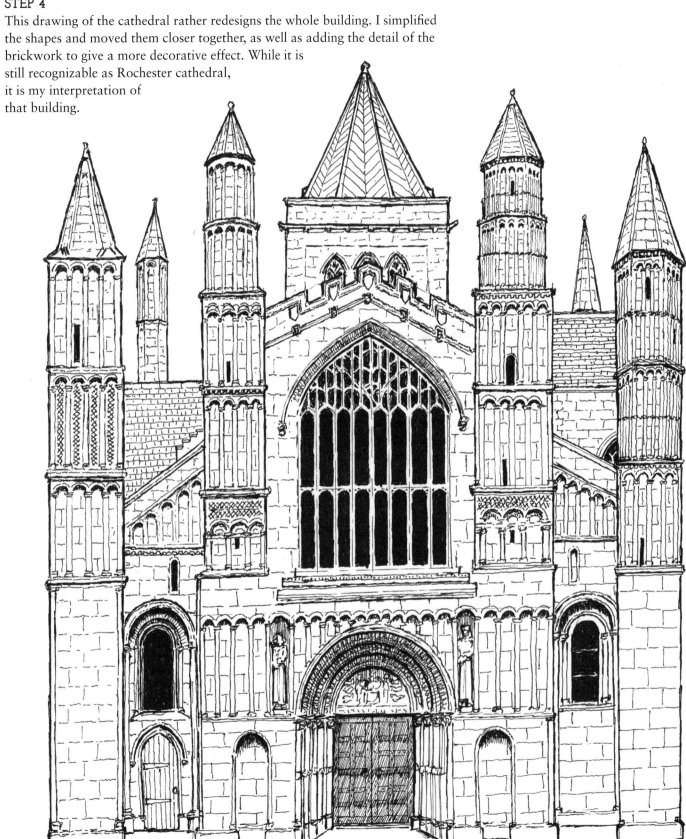

A fountain and pond

I found this subject in a formal garden – a water feature in which the water filled up a large bowl in the middle of a pond and gently dribbled over the edge, creating a circular area of splashes. The design and build of the bowl and pond seemed very precise and the whole view had an elegant, calming quality to it.

STEP 1
First draw the outlines of the scene quite simply, showing the pergola and hedgerows behind the pond as well.

STEP 2
Start to add some sketchy detail and tone to your drawing, identifying the darkest areas of the water and back wall beyond the pergola. Keep your tones light at this stage.

STEP 3

Work up your drawing with darker tones and detail to create a picture of the lush, peaceful scene on your paper. Note the different types of marks I have used for the various areas of the garden: scribbly marks for the leaves, rough lines for grasses, short, sharp lines for the tiling in the foreground and small waves on the surface of the pond itself.

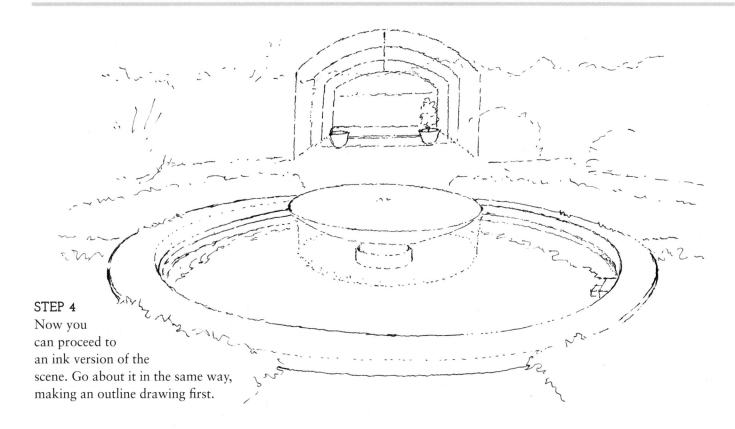

STEP 4
Now you
can proceed to
an ink version of the
scene. Go about it in the same way,
making an outline drawing first.

STEP 5
Work up the image texturally to give it more solidity. Make a conscious effort to slow down your drawing in order to derive maximum enjoyment from making the marks on the page. Don't worry about the final result; it's the process that matters.

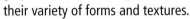

Cornucopia

For the final drawing in this book, I chose to return to my kitchen and celebrate one of the great pleasures in life: food. Taking a whole range of fruit and vegetables – a pumpkin, a plait of garlic, artichokes, potatoes, onions, courgettes and grapes – I made a design that would capture their variety of forms and textures.

STEP 1
First arrange your fruits and vegetables in an attractive mass on a flat surface and sketch them in. I placed mine quite low down and viewed them from above.

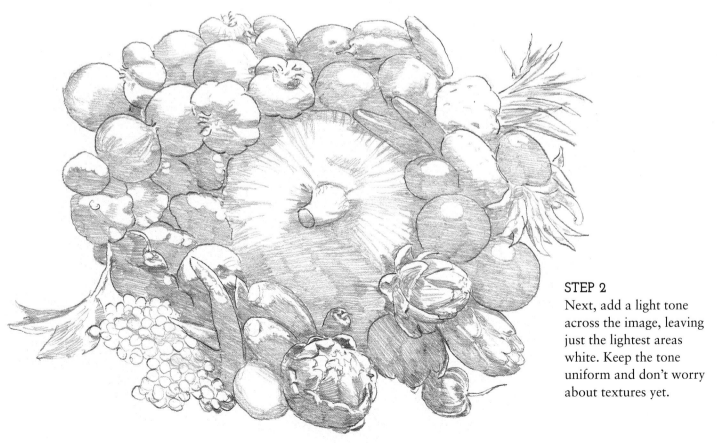

STEP 2
Next, add a light tone across the image, leaving just the lightest areas white. Keep the tone uniform and don't worry about textures yet.

STEP 3

Now draw up in as much detail as you can, using tone to build up the solidity of the objects. This is a slow process, because there are many different tones and textures in this group. The garlic bulbs can be defined with contour lines that follow their papery skins, whereas the potatoes have a speckled surface. Look carefully at each foodstuff to decide on your tonal approach.

STEP 4

You might be tempted to stop after making this first drawing, but I encourage you to trace it off and make another version in ink. You can use this version to achieve a decorative, patterned approach that really jumps out of the page. Be guided by the balance of your original drawing. Use different methods of hatching and dotting techniques, as I have done here. Sometimes, as in the onions and garlic, make the lines of hatching follow the shape of the object, but in the darker vegetables cross-hatch to get deeper textures.